TRUCKS

A to Z

by Christopher
Hernandez

SCHOLASTIC

For my teenage
grandparents, I love you
both in so many ways—
from A to Z!
—C.H.

ISBN 978-0-545-49110-5

12 11 10 9 8 7 6 5 4 3 2 1   12 13 14 15 16 17/0

Printed in the U.S.A.   40

First printing, September 2012

Design by Kay Petronio

Whether they are building, dumping, mixing, or smashing, trucks can do some amazing things. Let's hit the road to take a closer look at trucks from

A to Z

A

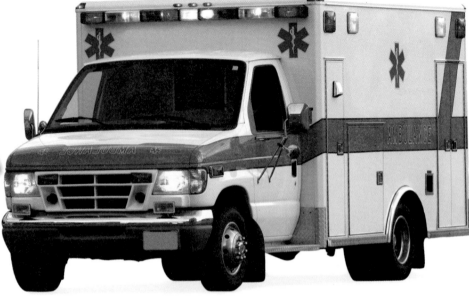

Ambulance

Ambulances **transport** sick or injured people to hospitals. They also have medicines and machines on board to help those people during the ride.

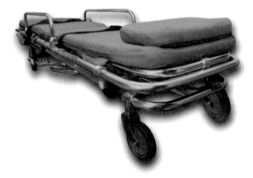

Armored truck

These trucks have thick walls of strong metal. They are used to protect some*thing*, like money, or some*one*, like a policeman.

Backhoe

A backhoe is used to excavate, or dig, holes and trenches. The part of the arm that holds the bucket is called the dipper.

Bulldozer

This powerful tractor has a large shovel at the front called a blade. It is used for pushing dirt, gravel, or other materials.

C

Concrete mixer

Concrete mixers can do two jobs at once. They make concrete as well as carry it to wherever it is needed.

- - - - - - - - - -

Cherry picker

Cherry pickers are used for more than just collecting fruit. Many different workers use them to go places their ladders cannot reach.

- - - - - - - - - - -

Delivery truck

These trucks are used to deliver all sorts of goods. The first delivery trucks were created to replace horse-drawn wagons.

Dump truck

Dump trucks have a large box that is used to haul and dump material. Heavy-duty dump trucks can carry up to 200 tons

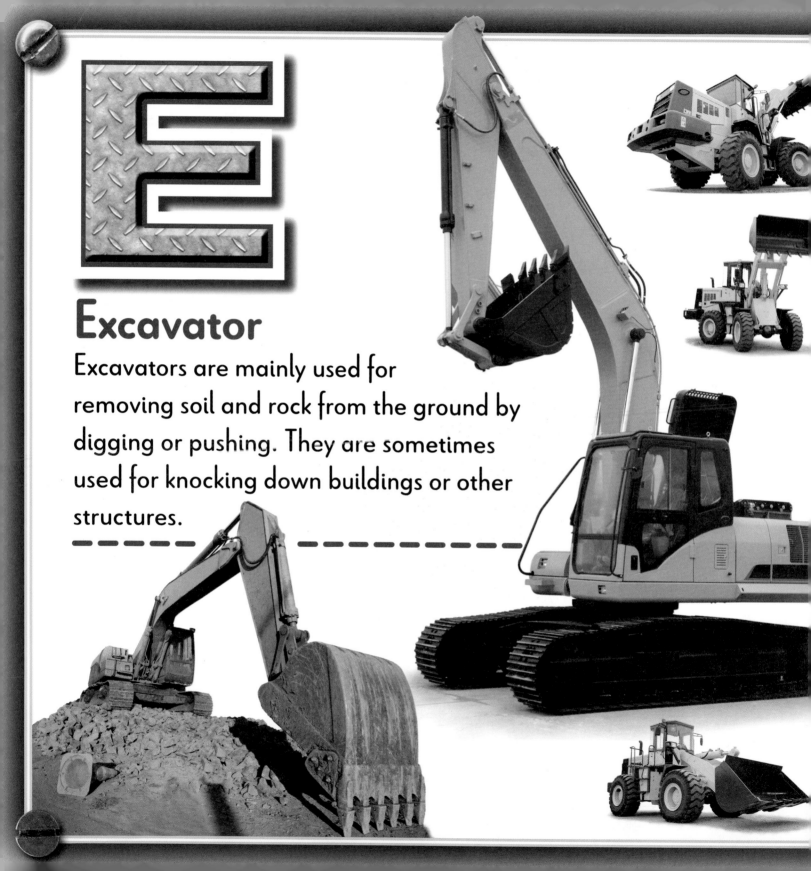

Excavator

Excavators are mainly used for removing soil and rock from the ground by digging or pushing. They are sometimes used for knocking down buildings or other structures.

Fire truck

Firefighters use many different types of trucks to help them fight fires. Many fire trucks have their own ladders, and some even carry their own supply of water.

Forklift

A forklift is a small truck used for moving heavy objects short distances. It is named after the two prongs, or forks, at its front.

Garbage truck

Garbage trucks are used to take trash to a landfill. Some have prongs that can pick up trash, but others need people to load them up.

Hay loader

This truck is used to move bales, or piles, of hay. Using a special claw, it can pick up the bales and load them onto other trucks.

Ice-cream truck

These trucks sell all sorts of ice cream—from sundaes to milk shakes. In warm weather, they can be heard driving around neighborhoods playing their catchy songs.

Jingle truck

Jingle trucks are colorfully decorated vehicles found mostly in Central Asia. They earned their name from the noise made by their jingling ornaments.

K

Knuckle boom truck

This truck has a crane for loading and unloading. The crane bends at the middle, or knuckle, just like a finger.

Loaders

Loaders are a type of excavator. With their buckets, they can pick up materials like dirt and rocks, and dump them somewhere else.

Lunch truck

Lunch trucks are like reverse drive-throughs because they bring food to people. On board, they have stoves and other appliances needed to cook food.

M

Monster truck

Monster trucks are pickups with massive wheels. At car shows, they can be found making huge jumps or driving over and crushing smaller cars.

News truck

These trucks are used by reporters to bring us news from many different locations. They help news shows report on breaking, or live, news.

Oversize-load truck

These trucks do some of the heaviest lifting of any vehicle. They transport heavy things, including other vehicles and even pre-built homes.

OVERSIZE LOAD

OVERSIZE LOAD

Pickup

These trucks are used for picking up and delivering smaller cargo. The open area at the back is called a bed.

Postal truck

The post office uses these trucks to deliver mail to your home. The United States Postal Service has the world's largest fleet of vehicles.

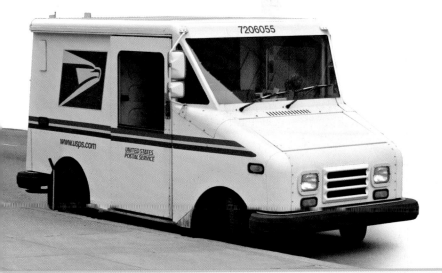

Quarry truck

A quarry is a place where rocks are removed from the earth. Quarry trucks are heavy-duty dump trucks that are used to transport these rocks.

Recreational vehicle

These trucks, also known as motor homes or RVs, are like houses on wheels. They have a bedroom, kitchen, and sometimes even a bathroom.

Road roller

Road rollers are used to create roads. Once concrete or **asphalt** has been poured, these trucks drive over it to smooth the ground.

S

Snowplow

These trucks are used to clear roads and streets after big snowstorms. Like a bulldozer, they plow with a large scoop that pushes the snow.

Street sweeper

Every day, street sweepers drive down city roads, cleaning up trash. With their spinning brooms, they can sweep up all kinds of garbage.

Tanker truck

These long trucks have tanks that can carry all sorts of liquids, from milk to gasoline.

Tow truck

When cars get a flat tire or have other kinds of accidents, tow trucks are able to move them to a safe place for repairs.

Utility truck

These vehicles are perfect for people who need a lot of storage. They help electricians and other workers keep their tools and equipment organized.

Vacuum truck

Whenever there is a big mess that needs cleaning, these trucks are up for the job. Their powerful vacuums can suck up everything from water and dirt to mud and sewage.

W

Wheelie truck

This vehicle is usually found at car shows and other events. They perform a trick called a wheelie by popping up and resting only on their back wheels.

X-ray truck

Like the X-ray at your doctor's office, these trucks use X-rays to check other trucks, cars, and containers for illegal items.

Y

Yard spotter

Yard spotters are used to move trailers around terminals and ports. With a small cab and large windows, they are designed to be easier to operate than other trucks.

Zamboni™

The Zamboni™ is an ice resurfacer that was created in 1949. By laying down a layer of water, which quickly freezes, this truck can clean and smooth the surface of an ice rink.

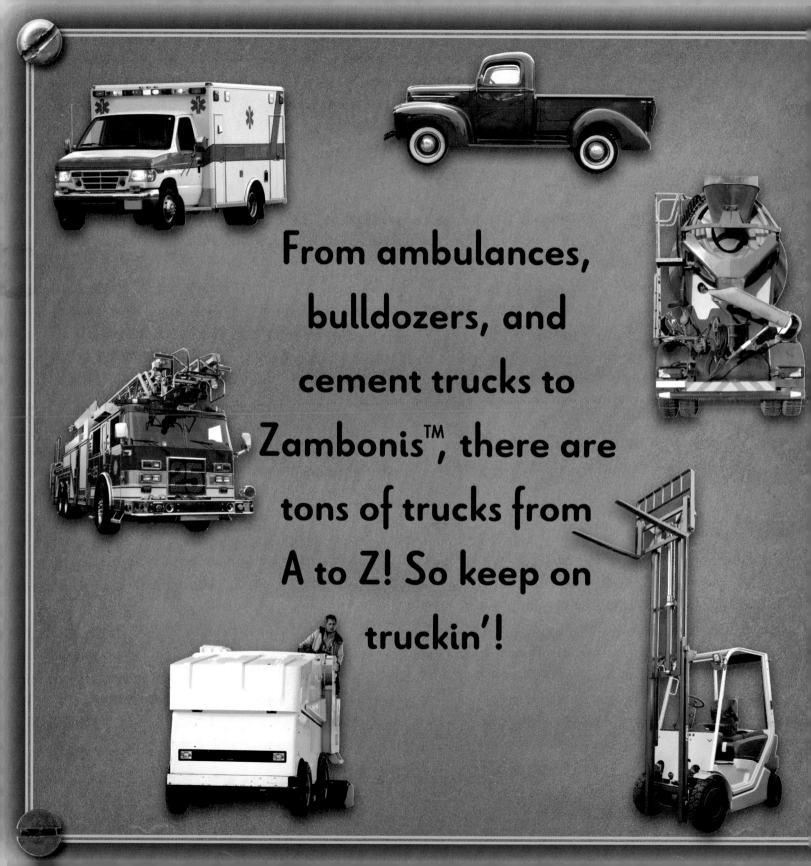

From ambulances, bulldozers, and cement trucks to Zambonis™, there are tons of trucks from A to Z! So keep on truckin'!

Glossary

Appliances—Machines used to perform a special task

Asphalt—A special mixture used for creating roads and other flooring

Excavate—To dig material out of the ground

Landfill—An area used specifically for keeping garbage and waste

Sewage—Waste found in sewers

Transport—To carry from one place to another

Tractor—A short truck with a cab for the driver

Quarry—A place where stones or other materials are dug out of the earth